The Voice  Women's

Wisdom

Dedicated to my granddaughter Aria.

Table of Contents

Introduction

I have been fascinated with the expressive and healing potential of the voice since I was a young voice student. Just like when they say the eyes are the window to the soul, I believe that the voice is how we express that soul and offers us a deeper experience of our inner landscape. Our voice is a living instrument and is one of the most powerful tools we have to communicate with others - it carries our life-force energy! The sound of our voice expresses who we are and what we are feeling and thinking. It tells a story of our inner world.

Our voice communicates so much about us. By listening to a person speak, you can tell their age, sex, emotional mood, where they're from, how much education they've had, what they had for dinner...well maybe not! The tone of your voice can also engender feelings of love, trust and respect, or dislike, suspicion and contempt.

Your voice can also be a holographic representation of your state of health, as shown through the new science of human bioacoustics. Our heart also has a voice, and I believe the bridge from the heart to the voice is the key to empowerment and effective communication, and I'm going to share some groundbreaking information on the heart that will support this. We will also explore the importance of learning to listen at a deeper level - there is a cycle of energy in the voice/ear/brain connection that helps to maintain wellness. I also will share concepts that will open up a greater awareness of your body as a vibrant instrument of expressive communication and a tool for connecting to our divine aspect.

Throughout this book I have provided links to videos and websites that illustrate, support and add to the impact of the concepts that are shared. You can access the links at:

https://www.ruthratliff.com/voice-of-women-s-wisdom.

Whether it is through speaking truth clearly or singing our hearts out, we all have the right to express our authentic selves. Our voice is one of the most powerful tools we have for heart-centered communication and healing. It is a vibrant instrument that can have a direct effect on our physical, emotional and spiritual health and well being.

Our sacred voice is a unique gift we are each given at birth to allow life to move through us and express itself! Spiritual teacher Sonia Choquette wrote a song called "Inner Voice" and the lyrics say it all: "you have a holy voice inside you."

Chapter 1: My Story

One of my most poignant memories as a young teenager was sitting with my mom and little brother playing cards, freezing in the dark with our coats on. It was winter, and my dad had come home drunk and got on a bender about one of us accidentally leaving a door open, so he ran around and opened up all the doors and windows and turned the power off, yelling at the top of his voice all the while. I remember my mom trying to keep us as quiet as possible, in the hope that dad would calm down and fall asleep...

A couple of years later on Christmas Eve my dad and I were arguing and when I worked up the courage to say "you're an alcoholic," I got slapped across the face. I ran out of the house and my boyfriend picked me up for last-minute shopping. That was the last time I saw my dad alive. Christmas morning, a somber State Trooper came to break the news that he had died in a car accident on a snowy highway at 2 a.m. The loss of a parent is one of the most traumatic experiences we can go through, but the grief I should have felt never happened. I just felt hollow.

I also remember the emotionally painful "silent treatments" my mom would inflict on us for days sometimes, without ever telling us what we did to hurt her feelings. There was no talking to clear things up - we were not taught to express feelings, or talk about problems and disagreements. So a couple of decades later when my mom was told that she had cancer and only had a few months to live, she chose not to tell my brother and I. We only found out at the hospital the day she died. Less than a year later my brother, who had been diagnosed as bi-polar, committed suicide after spiraling down into a depression triggered by our mother's death. I remember hiding in my clothes closet, from what I had no idea - I just couldn't stand being in my body.

"They say what doesn't kill you makes you stronger - I should be able to bench press a Buick by now!"

It has been a long journey of dealing with the anger and abandonment to a place of forgiveness. I love to read, so self-help books were like balm on my emotional wounds. I also sought out the help of a wonderful grief counselor, who gave me permission to release the pain by hitting pillows and yelling at the top of my voice!

This family dynamic created a great fear in me of speaking my mind. This fear stopped me from sticking up for myself in episodes of sexual harassment at work, kept me in bad relationships way too long, and I still feel it in the pit of my stomach during confrontational conversations.

The journey to find my own voice started at age 13 when my mom enrolled me in singing lessons. My first teacher opened up another world of expression to me through the beautiful music of classical voice. Each subsequent teacher gave me opportunities to peel away the layers of protection that I had surrounded myself with. As I became more and more comfortable with opening up my sound and sharing it with others, I developed a sense of empowerment and self-esteem that I can only attribute to learning to own the power of my voice. I have since made it my life work to learn as much as I could about the amazing world of vocal sound and it's myriad healing and spiritual applications.

The experience of coaching voice for the past 20 years has also been a profound journey of self-discovery. While I was honing the art of teaching voice, I was also being taught by my students and clients. They reflected my ego back at me, and taught me how to be a really good listener, and that there is strength in vulnerability. And they made me laugh, lots of laughter and joy sharing breakthroughs and yes, tears of frustration as well. I always tell my students that the journey of voice will open them up in unexpected ways, and it has!

"How wonderful is the human voice - it is indeed the organ of the soul!" Longfellow

Part 1

Women's Barriers to Full Self Expression

Chapter 2:
Women's Voices Through History

Women's voices throughout history have been minimized, criticized, blocked or shut down by collective societal consciousness, which has created physical and emotional holding patterns in how we express ourselves. Expression is a creative gift that we are all born with, and women's historical lack of rights have made us doubt our wise and intuitive voice. Freedom of speech is a basic right that is sometimes taken for granted in our country, and almost denied completely in others. Being able to speak and to be heard and respected, whether it be in a family or global situation, is essential to feeling valued and developing a sense of ourselves. Our collective "voices" are meant to be shared from a place of empowerment to facilitate meaningful change in the world.

"Women's voices are being suppressed all over the world," said Susan Rice, former U.S. Ambassador to the United Nations. She said this in response to the practice of some foreign nations that put women in jail for speaking out. While not suppressed in democracies, women's voices are still not fully heard, and I believe that the collective consciousness and energy of that suppression affects us all.

In this paradigm, when men speak, they are subconsciously given more respect and weight. Most women tend to speak from a position of inclusion, collaboration and community, which is sometimes judged as weakness. Deborah Tannen, a professor of linguistics, says there are two languages: the masculine "report talk" and the feminine "rapport talk." Along a similar line, a study in 2012 (Link 1) found that people prefer a leader, either man or woman, with a lower pitched voice. However, women with lower voices are not always considered as attractive as their higher voiced counterparts, and we all know how much weight is put on that. The same study showed that a higher pitched voice in either man or woman does not engender the same feelings of respect and security. Confused yet? This thin verbal line women have been walking has gotten us tongue tied; wanting to speak up, but afraid of being judged. Developing a more balanced, rather than judgmental or egoic listening ability, would be an important first step towards hearing each other fully. Embracing both the masculine and feminine aspects in ourselves is crucial to create balance in our inner and outer worlds.

Marie, a young professional woman I worked with, didn't think she was being taken seriously at work. After a few weeks of our time together, she told me that not only was she more comfortable speaking at meetings, but she noticed that she felt lighter and was laughing more. **So let's explore some concepts and tools that will help to give you a new perspective on your voice, to help release some of those negative holding patterns!**

"It took me quite a long time to develop a voice, and now that I have it, I am not going to be silent." Madeline Albright

Part 2
Your Amazing Voice

Chapter 3: Overview

I share <u>this video</u> (Link 2) with all my clients just to show them how amazing their voice really is! Four singers, two female, two male, sing the beautiful song, Hear Us and Have Mercy, but with a twist...all you see are their vocal cords! Through the magic of a fiber-optic laryngoscope, you can view the vocal cords in action. What I am struck by in this video is the intelligence in this system. The breath comes up, creating air pressure that causes the cords to vibrate so quickly you cannot see it with the naked eye; changes in pitch and dynamics happen as if by magic, and all you have to do is have an intention to make sound!

Did you know that your voice is as unique as your fingerprint? There has never been and will never be another one like yours! Did you also know that you are an instrument? Yes, your voice is intrinsically connected to your whole body.

Almost every religion, race and country have incorporated vocal sounds into their healing and spiritual rituals - joining voices with others is a bonding experience. When you disown or disconnect from your voice, you create a block in your flow of energy. How much more empowering would it be to respect and celebrate the sacred gift of our voice!

Why do we use our voices?

To feel good

To celebrate

To communicate

To be creative

To connect with other people

To heal ourselves

To pray

To connect to our souls

We vocalize because something inside us needs to be expressed. Vocal sound moves us in inexplicable ways. It is a unique gift that we are given to allow life to reveal itself through us. From the time we are born, we have the need to make sound with our voices. Even before we utter words, we are giving voice to our hearts with simple melodies. So let's explore the amazing instrument that is your voice!

Chapter 4: Cymatics

Cymatics **(Link 3)** *is the study of visible sound vibrations,* and it has evolved our understanding of how sound affects all of us. We've all heard how singing a very high note can shatter a glass, or the sound of a violin can move grains of sand; well, the cells of our bodies, minds and spirits are affected the very same way by sound vibrations, especially the ones from our own voice! This study affirms that everything we perceive is continuously vibrating at it's own rate.

A device was developed in 2002 called a CymaScope, that can make sound visible in an entirely amazing way. The device uses a video camera to film the effect of a particular sound frequency or vocal vibration on water. Each frequency or pitch makes a complex, unique geometric pattern, that would put a snowflake to shame! These resonance patterns are directly related to the geometric figures found in nature. This instrument offers an exciting opportunity to examine the hidden world of sound and vibration. Video recordings have been made of the human voice in the cymascope, and they are called voice mandalas. A mandala is a spiritual and ritual symbol in Hinduism and Buddhism, representing the universe.

From cymascope.com: *"The beautiful geometry in your voice is unique to you because your body consists of a delicate tracery of energy, arranged layer upon layer, frequency upon frequency. Your voice emits these frequencies when you speak or sing, bathing you and everyone in your vicinity with this sound template that is yours alone."*

Experience your sacred voice! (Link 4)

Chapter 5: Sound Vibrations

We all know the phrase "good vibrations." Think of how you feel when a very loud truck roars up the road past your house, or you burn the toast and the smoke alarms go off (just happened to me recently), or when you are walking on the beach listening to the waves, or the sound of a baby laughing. You may have heard of experiments where two plants are exposed to either acid rock or classical music. No mystery which plant died!

The use of the voice as a healing medium goes back thousands of years. The fields of music therapy and sound healing are based on how we respond to vibrations. Sound healing employs the use of the voice, as well as crystal or metal singing bowls, tuning forks and gongs. It is a practice that facilitates balancing the vibration of the body, mind and spirit. There are thousands of sound healing practitioners worldwide, attesting to the profound nature of this modality.

"If you want to find the secrets of the universe,
think in terms of energy, frequency and vibration."

Nikola Tesla

Everything has an optimum range of vibration that is known as resonance. This vibration or frequency is measured in hertz, or cycles per second. A frequency of 1 Hz is one cycle per second. For example, the piano note middle C is 262 Hz, which means it vibrates 262 times per second. So let's take this a step further - the adult female voice vibrates at about 200 Hz. A healthy human body frequency is lower at approximately 70 Hz. Think about it; the human body is about 60% water - that means *you are literally bathing the cells of your body in higher vibrations every time you speak, tone, or sing!*

432Hz is an ancient tuning that is mathematically consistent with the universe - it is know as the "scientific tuning." Music based on 432Hz (Link 5) is thought to transmit beneficial healing energy, because it is a pure tone fundamental to nature.

Chapter 6: Bioacoustics

Some years back, my husband and I went to an open house for a very unusual business called the Davis Center for Sound. I was so excited by the work they were doing at this center, I wanted to get a job there! The director introduced us to the up and coming modality called Human Bioacoustics (Link 6). Basically, you speak into a microphone connected to a computer program that analyzes your voice in a voiceprint that looks like a graph with highs and lows. These variations in the graph indicate issues with your body, like a deficiency in a vitamin, or some illness. Of course I had to try it, so we found a practitioner in our area and made an appointment. I just had blood work done some weeks before, so I had a baseline for comparison. When I got the results of the voice print, they *exactly* matched the results of my blood work! The practitioner then programmed specific balancing frequencies into a "tone box," for me to listen to several times a week. One of the imbalances was insomnia, and I noticed that I was sleeping better after this treatment.

Imagine a world where we diagnose and treat with sound frequencies that allow the body to return to a natural state of coherence and energetic health!

"Each person possesses unique harmonics of frequency that can be expressed through the voice. However, when these complex frequencies of the body become unbalanced, the voice primarily reflects this altered state, and the body manifests it as dis-stress or dis-ease at the structural and biochemical levels." Sharry Edwards, Founder of Human Bioacoustics

Part 3: Tools for Authentic Expression

Chapter 7: Kinesthetic Movement

We can use the body to empower and wake up the voice of our soul. I'd like to share with you some concepts and exercises to help you develop something called kinesthetic awareness of your body while you are speaking, humming or toning. Basically kinesthetic awareness is a sense of where your body is in space and how the different parts of your body are interacting with each other. It's being present to the sensations in your body.

We are meant to be very liquid in our movement so animation can move through our bodies, so we can live this fully expressed human experience allowing authentic sound to move through us. In the "real" world there are many times when our voices are shut down physically and emotionally, which can create a freezing of the fascial matrix. If we can release the holding patterns in our bodies, our voices will open up and free expression will follow.

So let's take a look at some tips to help you integrate kinesthetic awareness with movement.

- Stay present to the sensations in your body when you are sounding - speaking, singing, humming, crying, toning, etc.

- Notice how you breathe in between sentences or sounds. See if you can release your breath into the lower part of your body. Note: relax your abdominal muscles!

- See if you can have a background awareness of the parts of your body that are moving.

- Are your movements free or tense? If tense, can you release them with a deep belly breath?

- Try closing your eyes when speaking for a deeper awareness of the sound of your voice vibrating in your body.

- Hand movements are helpful as the hands are connected to the speech center of the brain!

This is not a quick fix but can be extremely effective in facilitating lasting change in how you experience your voice. The best way to strengthen your kinesthetic sense is to become aware of it in your day to day communication. Check out my video (Link 7) on developing kinesthetic awareness.

Chapter 8: Power Pose

Take an inventory of your body posture right now.
Are you trying to make yourself small by hunching or holding your arms, crossing your ankles, or spreading out. Social psychologist Amy Cuddy presented a TED Talk about what she calls "power posing," which is adopting a posture of confidence despite how you feel. Dr. Cuddy explains when someone is being powerful with us we tend to make ourselves smaller. She has found that women are much more likely to make themselves smaller as they feel less powerful than men in general.

Her study shows that body language not only affects how other people feel about you, but how YOU feel about yourself. The study tests measured hormonal levels. The results showed that actual physiological changes occur in the body that produce a boost to confidence and assertiveness. So our body language absolutely affects how we think and feel about ourselves. It gives new meaning to the phrase "fake it til you make it!" I have used this power pose or superhero stance with my students and clients with great results. Our posture is integral to not only supporting the vocal mechanism but it also has an effect on the way the voice is presented. I teach many young people who have not yet developed a sense of poise.

When I demonstrate the super hero pose for them you should see the looks I get - then they try it themselves, and their faces register their surprise when their voices ring with new found authority and presence!

Adopt these: "High Power" Poses (top row)

Avoid these: "Low Power" Poses (bottom row)

(images courtesy of A. Cuddy, Harvard University)

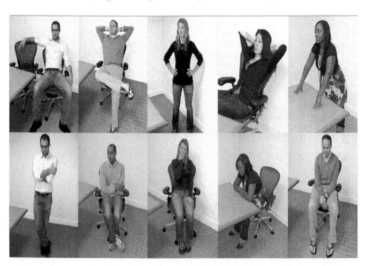

Chapter 9: Humming

Would you think that something so simple as a hum could improve the state of your health? Science is starting to catch up with evidence of the therapeutic effects of the vibrations of our voices. A simple hum can lower blood pressure and heart rate, facilitate the release of endorphins and melatonin, increase lymphatic circulation and increase oxygen in cells. Humming is an ancient practice that has been used in spiritual disciplines to aid in the connection with the divine. The humming of mantras during meditation has been shown to increase mental clarity and grounding.

I have been reading a great book by Jonathan Goldman called "The Humming Effect," (Link 8) and it has inspired me to hum every day! I've been listening to meditation music in the car and just hum on single comfortable pitches for about 10 minutes or so. I definitely notice feeling calmer, more positive and throat centered afterwards. You don't need to listen to music while you hum but I think it deepens the experience. This video (Link 9) is one of my favorites!

Humming is a powerful way to release stuck energy, especially in your throat chakra. It also facilitates the release of oxytocin, the happy hormone! Check out this YouTube video (Link 10) that walks you through a humming session. No wonder why people are always depicted as being happy while they hum!

There is also something called the Humming Bee Breath which originated in India. This is where you hum while covering your ears, which intensifies the experience of the vibrations in your head and body. It's also a wonderful way to deepen your breathing which also has amazing health benefits. Speaking of bees, a few scientists are exploring the healing properties of the sound of a hive of bees!

Chapter 9: Toning

The first time I was introduced to toning was at a weekend retreat called "Soul Song" in the Catskills of New York State (Another first during the retreat was sharing a coed bathroom which I will not go into here!) In one of the sessions there were about 50 of us sitting in a circle and toning the chakra vowel sounds. The experience of being surrounded by the force of the vibrations released something in me, and opened a floodgate of tears that washed away some of the grief I had been holding inside. It was one of the most profound healing experiences that I had had up to that point.

Toning is sounding on extended vowel sounds to feel the resonance in specific parts of your body called the chakras or energy centers. In ancient Sanskrit, Hebrew and Chinese the vowel sounds are considered to be sacred. Like other meditative practices, toning can reduce stress and release pent up emotions as well as developing your voice-ear connection. Toning has a kind of visceral feel to me where I can just "be" with no judgment or extraneous thoughts.

There is a wealth of information online about toning the chakras - I like this video by musician Johnny Booth who walks you through a toning session (Link 11). Even if you stay on the same pitch for the duration of the exercise, what matters most is your intention while you are toning. Remember, everyone can do this - you don't have to be able to "sing" to tone. I like to hum and tone together sometimes, depending on how I feel. Allow yourself be creative and playful with your voice! Remember when you were a child and you didn't think twice before making funny sounds?

"Toning is an activity that releases and allows the natural flow of energy to move through one's body." Tuning the Human Instrument by Steven Halpern.

Chapter 10: Primal Voice

Studies have been done regarding non-verbal communication or primal sounds. Are you ready for a shock? Well, these studies show that when explaining how we feel, only 7% of the words we use have an effect on the listener. Body language comes in at 55% and tone of voice at 38%. So you could essentially gesture and grunt and get your point across effectively!

Your primal voice is a reflexive organic sound production which includes crying, yelling, calling and whining. When you cried as a baby neural pathways were developed that connected to your larynx and became hardwired. From an early age the perception of our voices becomes colored with what we learn about making sounds. When children are expressing themselves with shouts, screams, whoops of joy and other primal sounds, what do we tell them? Sit down and be quiet! This probably causes us to develop unnecessary tensions based on fear of reprimand which also becomes hardwired in the brain. This may result in getting in our own way of creating free and authentic sounds as an adult. It is interesting to observe the resistance in my clients when we are working with organic sounds. They are surprised that something so simple as a cry or yell gets stuck in their throats!

One of my favorite authors, Dr. Christiane Northrup, says in her bestselling book, *Women's Body, Women's Wisdom*, "Making sounds is an important part of emotional release." In another story I read, a midwife said it was her experience that mothers who were more vocal in the birthing process had less complications than mothers who tried to control the desire to yell!

When you use a primal sound it elicits an "old brain" or limbic system response that is very reflexive and efficient. The cry is effective because it reconnects you with those free, instinctive sounds you made as a baby. I have been incorporating this cry or "wah" sound into my vocal practice and have also been sharing it with my clients. They are always amazed at how much easier it is to produce their sound when we pair the cry with traditional exercises. One client says she does the cry exercises on the way to work and feels more centered in her body when she arrives - ready for action!

Part 4

Owning Your Voice
And It's Wisdom

Chapter 11: The Voice of the Heart

"Listen to your heart" or "speak from your heart" are phrases that most of us are very familiar with. But what exactly does that mean, and what are we listening for, and does our heart really have a voice? The general idea that we are all taught is that the brain is the computer of the body controlling all the organs and systems and is the dominant "voice" of the body. However, new research is revealing that the heart actually sends more signals to the brain than the brain sends to the heart! These heart signals have an effect on emotions and cognitive faculties such as attention, perception, memory, and problem-solving. Also, the heart and brain are constantly communicating information back and forth. Researchers at the HeartMath Institute have found that the nerve center of the heart is so complex that it constitutes a "brain" on it's own - termed a "mini-brain." The heart also produces neurotransmitters and hormones previously thought to only be produced by the brain, one of which is oxytocin - the love hormone!

As if that wasn't enough, the heart is about 100,000 times stronger electrically and up to 5000 times stronger magnetically than the brain. It produces a measurable electromagnetic field called a torus field which radiates out about 3 to 4 feet and reacts with other people, animals, nature and our environment!

"From our research at the HeartMath Institute, we've concluded that intelligence and intuition are heightened when we learn to listen more deeply to our own heart. It's through learning how to decipher messages we receive from our heart that we gain the keen perception needed to effectively manage our emotions in the midst of life's challenges. The more we learn to listen to and follow our heart intelligence, the more educated, balanced and coherent our emotions become. Without the guiding influence of the heart we easily fall prey to reactive emotions such as insecurity, anger, fear and blame as well as other energy-draining reactions and behaviors."

You know that feeling when your "heart is full," you really do feel like there is a fullness in your chest. Most of us have suffered the pain of a broken heart - didn't it feel like it was really broken? When people point to themselves, they don't point at their head, they point to their heart...and isn't there a sense of something in your heart when you're faced with a difficult decision? These are all times when your heart is speaking to you. It is an organ of emotional intelligence and if you learn how to listen, it can also guide you!

Speaking from our heart means speaking our truth, our authentic feelings, being present in the moment. It takes courage to birth those feelings into words, squeezing them from your heart to your voice. I think we've all experienced the feeling of words "sticking" in our throats. We all expend a lot of life energy tiptoeing carefully through conversations, saying one thing and meaning another, trying not to offend or inflame, fearful of reaction. It's exhausting to try to sanitize our feelings before they come out of our mouths.

One of the things that has helped me free up my voice when it feels stuck, is simply to take a deep breath and release it on a sigh, with my hands over my heart. Since our voice literally is carried on our breath, the sigh can move the "stuck" throat energy.

I read the book *The Four Agreements* by Don Miguel Ruiz a number of years ago. The most impacting agreement to me was "be impeccable with your word" - not only the spoken word, but the unspoken words or thoughts we use against ourselves. If you trust that the heart's intelligence will guide your words (and thoughts) and truly listen to it's voice, it will empower you to connect with your divine self.

HeartMath offers a guided technique to get you into a state of coherence to regulate your thoughts and emotions to connect to your heart's intuitive intelligence. (Link 12)

It's no accident that the word *"courage"* comes from the French word *"cur"* which means heart. Courage is indeed what it takes to move past fear and communicate from the heart without defensiveness or protective measures. Sure you might get hurt, but what you gain by having the courage to make yourself vulnerable to speak your truth is priceless.

"You can't get to courage without walking through vulnerability." Brene Brown

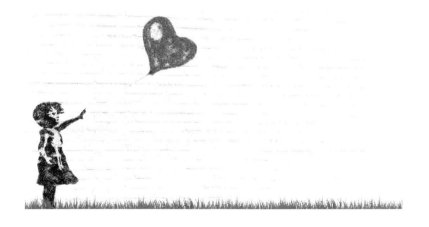

Chapter 12: Intuitive Voice

We all have had the experience of thinking of someone only to have them text or call shortly afterwards or come to find out they were sick or in an accident. Whether it's that gut feeling that defies logic or the heart feeling that takes us by surprise, intuition is universal to us all. Learning to develop and trust our intuitive intelligence is more important now than it ever has been before. We are bombarded daily with a deluge of information from various sources. Our natural intuitive intelligence is really all we need to know to guide us as to what is in our best interest. It can help us to navigate our life experience and the myriad forms of information that we are exposed to. Your intuitive voice speaks to you in many ways. Here's some of the methods that I've experienced, and I'm sure you have too!

- **Inner voice** - this is the "still, small voice" that is somewhat similar to my head babble, but has a different quality, like a nudge. I get a lot of these "nudges" while driving - like write an e-book, reach out to a friend, or watch out for that other car! I remember when I was seventeen I had broken up with my boyfriend Tim and felt terrible about hurting him. One evening a few weeks later, I was suddenly overcome with this unexplainable urge to go to the garage where he worked on his car. I drove there and somehow knew that I didn't want him to see me, so I parked in the lot next door. When I peeked in the window, I saw him in an embrace with another girl and immediately felt relief wash over me - taking away my guilt feelings. I was in a kind of dreamy state driving home, amazed at the force that had guided me there.

- **Inner knowing** - Sometimes there are no thoughts or images - we just know. This is an amazing feeling that is probably very foreign to most of us. It certainly was to me in this next story that happened about a decade later. My brother, who I told you about earlier, called me at work to ask if I would be mad at him if he committed suicide. Totally distraught, I said I was coming over after work to talk and I would bring dinner. I remember being at the Chinese restaurant and grabbing sets of chopsticks but putting one back because I knew Bill was gone - I just knew. Another time years later I applied for a job closer to home. After the interview I knew beyond a shadow of a doubt that I had the job, even after the director called and told me that he had given the position to someone else. The next day the director called back and offered the job to me because the other person had declined.

- **You actually hear a voice** - I did once when I was driving - it said "look right." Someone ran a red light as I was going through an intersection and I had just enough time to jam on my brakes and avoid what could have been a serious accident. Another time one of my co-workers at this new job asked if I knew someone who could teach her daughter voice lessons, and before I could think, a voice that did not feel like my own answered, "sure, I can!" So I said, "I guess I can..." and that was the start of my voice studio.

- **Heart or gut feeling** - That sinking feeling in the pit of your stomach, or that little flutter in your heart is trying to tell you something. When you meet someone for the first time, don't you usually get a heart feeling about them? Can't you feel it when some place has a good vibe? After I opened my voice studio, I put an ad in the paper for an accompanist. Out of about 15 applicants that I spoke with on the phone, I had a really good heart feeling about this one guy who is now my husband! We went on to open a joint music studio and performed together for many years. There definitely was an intuitive guiding force in my life that led me to become a voice teacher and meet my husband!

Call it what you will, there is an invisible connection between all of us that defies logic. Dr. Wayne Dyer has called it the "infinite field of energy." Quantum physics calls it the "unified field." This connection calls us to open our ears to a more mindful listening, suspending our doubts and fears - listening from a deeper, more receptive place. Remember, we are all connected through vibration, and the energy of our bodies is "tuned in" to the that field and is listening, even when we are not!

"Intuition is real - vibes are real - energy doesn't lie. Tune in."

Chapter 13: Compassionate Listening

When was the last time you remember really listening to someone, or having someone listen to you, or listening to your inner voice? Most people want to be listened to but few know the art of listening, especially listening with compassion. Of course listening starts with the ears, and I always tell my clients that the ears are an integral part of the voice. A recent discovery tells us that the voice-ear-brain connection is a subtle energy system within the body.

In her book The Cycle of Sound: A Missing Energetic Link, Dr. Dorinne Davis writes *"the **voice** reflects and impacts what the **ear** hears, emits and processes, and what the **brain** perceives, interprets, and relays to the body. The entire process is based upon the body's response to sound vibration."*

The discovery of this process gives us a greater understanding of ourselves and our connection to others, and enlarges the importance of listening in communication.Tuning in to the sounds in our environment can be a helpful first step towards a deeper experience of listening. A few years ago I attended a sound healing workshop, and the teacher had us all sit outside for a while, and just listen to the ambient sounds in the neighborhood. We were all surprised at how many sounds we could hear just by listening with intention, and amazed at all the ones we tune out!

Learning to listen to our thoughts, feelings and inner voice, as talked about in the previous chapters, can help gain clarity in our relationship to ourselves, without which it would be difficult to improve our communication with others. Meditative vocal practices can open your awareness to your higher self which can guide you to a deeper understanding.

We all know people who interrupt or jump to conclusions - they are listening only to what's on the surface. Generally we want to be understood more than we want to understand, and getting our point across becomes the primary goal. Why should we listen to them if they don't listen to us?

Active listening is defined as: *"the act of mindfully hearing and attempting to comprehend the meaning of words spoken by another in a conversation or speech."*

Compassionate listening means to shift the focus away from ourselves, and on to the other to try to understand what they are saying from *their* perspective, not *ours* and "reading between the lines." The quality of our listening is a skill which can be developed and strengthened, and can be a game-changer in your relationship with people. They become less defensive and more able to listen in return, because they feel that you *get* them, and isn't that what we all want?

Now imagine this on a larger scale, not just with your immediate circle. Can you feel how healing that would be on a global level? Listening can foster understanding, empathy and connection, and helps us to find the commonality in each other.

Chapter 14: Potential for Empowerment, Healing and Awakening

I think by now you are beginning to understand that your voice has an amazing potential to balance you physically, emotionally and spiritually. The scientific community is finally catching up with the possibility that we are able to therapeutically impact physical and emotional issues with sound. Quantum physics tells us that we exist in a field of energy, and matter is not as solid as it seems. Dr. Richard Gerber in <u>Vibrational Medicine</u> "We, as human organisms, are a series of interacting multidimensional subtle-energy systems, and that if these energy systems become imbalanced...these imbalances can be healed with the right frequency of vibrational medicine." Joshua Leeds, the author of *The Power of Sound* and an expert in the field of psychoacoustics, says "sound work is creating a frequency and vibration for someone that's conducive for him or her to heal."

In traditional Chinese Medicine, the voice is used as an instrument of release in order to shift the patient into a more enlivened state. I recently learned that an acupuncturist will listen to the tone of a patient's voice as one of the indicators of health. We have been aware for some time that illness is not only caused by toxins, germs or heredity, but also by the stress of dysfunctional ways of relating to ourselves and others. The sound healing approach, especially through the use of voice, has been shown to bring about changes in the mind and spirit, and facilitates the body's ability to heal itself.

More and more people are opening to the concept that we are beings of energy, and our voice is a powerful healing tool of vibration, which can realign and rebalance our "out of tune" energies. Edgar Cayce (the "sleeping prophet"), predicted that sound would be the medicine of the future.

"The body is held together by sound. The presence of disease indicates that some sounds have gone out of tune."

Deepak Chopra

Marianne Hughes of the Institute for Social Change wrote "Recently, the Dalai Lama caused a stir when at the peace conference in Vancouver he said that "the world will be saved by western women". I'm not entirely sure what he meant by that but I am wondering if when he travels across the globe and sees so many of our sisters impoverished and repressed he sees western women of all ages in a position to speak out for justice...to take loving care of the planet and its people."

I believe that most of us can sense that the balance of energy is shifting more to the feminine aspect - not of gender but quality, which is inherent in both men and women. I like to compare it to the right and left sides of our brains - the left side is more logical and linear, and the right side is emotional and creative. We all know people that seem too much one way or the other. We need to integrate both sides to strike a balance. This is the same regarding embracing the masculine/feminine aspects in all of us. It is wonderful that there is a more inclusive world emerging where both masculine and feminine approaches are valued, but like the layers of an onion, we are still peeling away and throwing off the layers of ancestral paradigms and ways of being.

As I wrote in Chapter 2, the powers of the feminine voice have been minimized and repressed for centuries, to the point where we do not value our natural abilities, sensitivities and intelligence. We sometimes give away our own power with words that are apologetic, people-pleasing or self-deprecating. Some of us find it difficult to ask directly for what we need, feeling selfish and self-centered. I believe the idea of being "all things to all people" which is actually written in the Bible at I Corinthians 9:19-23, has left an ancient imprint on women; not only in the world view, but how we view ourselves. Our own embodied voice is an integral path for facilitating change and empowerment! The voice is an incredibly powerful tool that can be wielded to hurt or to heal - it is also an ancient pathway to self-realization.

Listen with compassion to the voice of your heart and hear what it's telling you. Open your ears to your intuition for guidance on how to give voice to your needs and wants. Just listen… and as you heal and gain trust in the voice of your soul, you will find that your expression comes from a more empowered and authentic place. Something wonderful happens when we hum, tone, sing, or speak with intention; it awakens the voice of the wisdom our soul, and we begin to remember the beauty of who we are.

"While we each vibrate at our own frequency (sounding our 'individual note'), we are simultaneously participating in the greater symphony of life through our roles as dynamic receivers, transformers, and transmitters of thought."

Dr. Joe Dispenza

My heartfelt wish is that the concepts and tools I shared with you in this book will open your eyes to the magic of your voice, whether it be through thought, speech or singing! I hope it will help you to develop, strengthen and empower the expression of the sacred feminine aspect of your soul. Let's fall in love with our voices in all their myriad expressions, and remember and honor what we truly are...

Wise, Powerful, Loving and Divine!

YOU ARE SOMETHING DIVINE — MORE BEAUTIFUL AND GLORIOUS THAN YOU CAN POSSIBLY IMAGINE.

About the Author

"She should take voice lessons when she's older" said Ruth's kindergarten teacher to her Mom. This started her on a lifelong journey of discovery into the power of voice. Born in the Big Apple, Ruth became a Jersey girl when her parents wanted to move to the countryside. Growing up taking care of a horse, pony, chickens and ducks and working in the family garden opened Ruth's eyes to the magic of nature. Music and singing was always a big part of her life through school. She studied vocal performance and pedagogy at Mannes Music College in New York City, The New School for the Arts in Montclair, NJ, and Westminster Choir College in Princeton, NJ. Ruth has been a holistic voice coach for over 20 years, with a performance background encompassing musical theater, classical, jazz, pop and sacred genres. Since 1995, she and husband Jim have been welcoming students and clients to their home studio Jemini Music in Hope, NJ.

Ruth has been fascinated with the expressive and healing potential of the voice since she was a young voice student, and has a particular passion for the holistic, healing properties of our voices. She is currently pursuing a certification in vibrational sound practice, and has attended many workshops and courses on various types of sound healing. Also, Ruth is certified in Shoden Reiki Level I and is studying to become a

Level 2 practitioner. Her husband refers to her as the research queen, as one of her favorite places is in front of the computer googling the next interesting topic. If you can't find her there, she'll be working in their beautiful studio gardens looking for the garden fairies. Ruth loves reading, singing, interior decorating, making videos, gardening, bird watching, 80's rock, hunting for seashells and their sweet dachshund Baxter.

Visit her at www.ruthratliff.com.

LINKS

1. journals.plos.org/plosone/article?id=10.1371/journal.pone.0051216

2. https://www.youtube.com/watch?v=-XGds2GAvGQ

3. https://www.youtube.com/watch?v=GtiSCBXbHAg

4. https://www.youtube.com/watch?v=vN-n3Q9d6Q8&t=23s

5. https://www.youtube.com/watch?v=lU13sdrLQ-M

6. https://www.youtube.com/watch?v=b92TXSq5Plo

7. https://www.youtube.com/watch?v=DrczKvdv9Ow

8. https://www.healingsounds.com/product/the-humming-effect-book/

9. https://www.youtube.com/watch?v=slS8Qbj15TU

10. https://www.youtube.com/watch?v=zQQmsGaD2es

11. https://www.youtube.com/watch?v=tFnxLyzosvs

12. https://www.heartmath.org/resources/heartmath-tools/quick-coherence-technique-for-adults/

Made in the USA
Middletown, DE
21 September 2021